First World War
and Army of Occupation
War Diary
France, Belgium and Germany

1 INDIAN CAVALRY DIVISION
Divisional Troops
Divisional Ammunition Column
31 August 1914 - 31 December 1916

WO95/1170/3

The Naval & Military Press Ltd
www.nmarchive.com
Published in association with The National Archives

Published by

The Naval & Military Press Ltd

Unit 10 Ridgewood Industrial Park,

Uckfield, East Sussex,

TN22 5QE England

Tel: +44 (0) 1825 749494

www.naval-military-press.com

www.nmarchive.com

This diary has been reprinted in facsimile from the original. Any imperfections are inevitably reproduced and the quality may fall short of modern type and cartographic standards.

© Crown Copyright
Images reproduced by permission of The National Archives, London, England, 2015.

Contents

Document type	Place/Title	Date From	Date To
Heading	WO95/1170/3		
Heading	BEF 1 Ind. Cav. Div. Troops Ind. Div. Ammo. Col. RHA 1914 Aug To 1916 Dec		
War Diary		31/08/1914	06/10/1914
War Diary	Sialkot	09/10/1914	19/11/1914
War Diary	Orleans	19/11/1914	30/11/1914
Heading	War Diary of "B" Ammunition Column R.H.A. From 7-12-14 To 25-12-14 Volume I Pp 8 to 10		
War Diary		07/12/1914	25/12/1914
Heading	War Diary of Ammunition Column 1st Indian Cavalry Division January-December-1915		
Heading	War Diary of 1st Indian Cavalry Division Ammunition Column From 1st January 1915 To 31st January 1915		
War Diary		01/01/1915	31/01/1915
Heading	War Diary of "B" Ammunition Column R.H.A. 1st Indian Cavalry Division From 1st February 1915 To 24th/28th February 1915		
War Diary		01/02/1915	24/02/1915
Heading	War Diary of Divisional Ammunition Column, R.H.A. 1st Indian Cavalry Division From 2nd March 1915 To 31st March 1915		
War Diary		02/03/1915	27/03/1915
Heading	War Diary of Divisional Ammunition Column, 1st Indian Cavalry Division From 25th March 1915 To 31st March 1915		
War Diary		25/03/1915	27/03/1915
Heading	War Diary of Divisional Ammunition Column 1st Indian Cavalry Division From 1st April 1915 To 30th April 1915		
War Diary		03/04/1915	12/04/1915
War Diary	Rue-Du-Dormier	24/04/1915	24/04/1915
War Diary	Sylvester Cappel	25/04/1915	25/04/1915
War Diary	St Marie Cappel	28/04/1915	28/04/1915
Heading	War Diary of Ammunition Column; 1st Indian Cavalry Division From 1st May 1915 To 31st May 1915		
War Diary		02/05/1915	30/05/1915
Heading	War Diary of 1st Indian Cavalry Division Ammunition Column From 1st June 1915 To 31st July 1915		
War Diary	Quiestede	10/07/1915	10/07/1915
Heading	War Diary of 1st Indian Cavalry Divisional Ammunition Column From 1st August 1915 To 31st December 1915		
War Diary		01/08/1915	15/12/1915
Heading	War Diary of 1st Indian Cavalry Division Ammunition Column From 1st February 1916 To 29th February 1916		
War Diary		01/02/1916	29/02/1916
Heading	War Diary of 1st Indian Cavalry Division Ammunition Column From 1st March 1916 To 31st March 1916		
War Diary		01/03/1916	31/03/1916

Heading	War Diary of 1st Indian Cavalry Divisional Ammunition Column From 1st April 1916 To 30th April 1916		
War Diary		01/04/1916	30/04/1916
Heading	War Diary of 1st Indian Cavalry Divisional Ammunition Column From 1st May 1916 To 31st May 1916		
War Diary		01/05/1916	31/05/1916
Heading	War Diary of 1st Indian Cavalry Divisional Ammunition Column From 1st June 1916 To 30th June 1916		
War Diary		01/06/1916	30/06/1916
Heading	War Diary of 1st Indian Cavalry Divisional Ammunition Column From 1st July 1916 To 31st July 1916		
War Diary		01/07/1916	31/07/1916
Heading	War Diary of 1st Indian Cavalry Divisional Ammunition Column From 1st August 1916 To 31st August 1916		
War Diary		01/08/1916	31/08/1916
Heading	War Diary of Ammunition Column 1st Indian Cavalry Division From 1st September 1916 To 30th September 1916		
War Diary		01/09/1916	30/09/1916
Heading	War Diary of Ammunition Column 4th Cavalry Division (late 1st Ind. Divn.) From 1st October 1916 To 30th November 1916		
War Diary		01/10/1916	30/11/1916
Heading	War Diary of Ammunition Column, 4th Cavalry Division From 1st December 1916 To 31st December 1916		
Heading	War Diary of 4th Cavalry Divisional Ammunition Column From 1st December 1916 To 31st December 1916 (Volume I)		
War Diary		01/12/1916	31/12/1916

No 95/1170/3

BEF
1 IND. CAV. DIV. TROOPS

IND. DIV. AMMO. COL. KHA
1914 AUG to 1916 DEC

Army Form C. 2118.

"B" Ammunition Column WAR DIARY
R.H.A.
(Lt. T. C. Wilson) or
INTELLIGENCE SUMMARY.
(Erase heading not required.)

Instructions regarding War Diaries and Intelligence Summaries are contained in F. S. Regs., Part II, and the Staff Manual respectively. Title pages will be prepared in manuscript.

No 3 Section
A. G's Office at Base
I. E. Force
Passed to Genl S. Sectn
on 26-11-14

ADJUTANT GENERAL INDIA
25. NOV. 1914
BASE OFFICE

(1)

Hour, Date, Place.	Summary of Events and Information.	Remarks and references to Appendices.
9.a.m. August 31 Sept 4 1914.	Received orders to mobilise. All ranks recalled from leave by wire and recruits summoned to rejoin by letter.	A.C.W. per.
Sept. 2. 1914.	War establishment of Horse Artillery Ammn received. Reorganisation carried out. No extra horses or men were required. (Telegram No 83/1 (A.G.1.17)	ACW.
Sept 6 1914	All Officers directed to take their ord charges. Telegram No 2986/W/3 C.G.S.	ACW.
Sept 26 1914	Telegram No 618/R G.S.O. Cav. Div. I.E.F. "A" "Artillery will be issued with rifles at Port of disembarkation" Rifles had previously been returned to Arsenal Rawal Pindi.	ACW.
Sept 15. 1914	Mobilisation reported "Completed".	ACW.
Sept 30 1914	Telegram from Arsenal Karachi. 472 Shff. .303 ammunition will not be issued to ammunition Column.	ACW.
Oct. 6	No 2692.A. from Bde Maj. Cav. Bde. Orders to be ready to move by 18th Oct.	ACW.

Army Form C. 2118.

WAR DIARY
or
INTELLIGENCE SUMMARY.
(Erase heading not required.)

(2)

Hour, Date, Place.	Summary of Events and Information.	Remarks and references to Appendices.
Siallit Oct 9th 1914	Rec'd wire No 529 from Control, Simla, "2nd Cav. Bde. Ammn. Col. to leave SIALKOT for KIMARI on 11th inst."	AW.
Oct 11th	Left SIALKOT at 7.30 AM	AW.
Oct 13th	Arrived KARACHI at 1-45 P.M. went into camp. Embarked vehicles on S.S. City of Calcutta	AW.
Oct 14th	Embarked horses, mules & A.T. carts of both H.A. & S.&T. Corps. As accommodation for all the mules did not exist on the City of Calcutta, half were embarked on ONDA and SEALDA under O.C. 19th Lancers, taken on turn "Calcutta"	AW.
Oct 15th	276 boxes 13pr Q.F. Ammn: and placed in magazine on Calcutta. Staff 2nd Cav. Bde. & Q Battery R.H.A. also embarked during the day on SS City of Calcutta. That portion of deck allotted to "B" Ammn. Col. horses contained satisfactory accommodation with facilities for exercising	BW

Army Form C. 2118.

WAR DIARY
or
INTELLIGENCE SUMMARY.
(Erase heading not required.)

(3)

Hour, Date, Place.	Summary of Events and Information.	Remarks and references to Appendices.
Oct 16th 1914. 4 P.m.	Left Karachi [illegible]	MW
Oct 27th 1914.	Native Dr. Rhana Singh, died of Pneumonia on the City of Calcutta, H.T.	MW
Nov 8th 1914	One Horse died	MW
Nov 10th 1914	Arrived Marseilles, disembarked horses which remained on wharf for night, drew 8 rifles, & ammunition for these rifles & 24 rounds per revolver also service clothing for men from Ordnance, the S.A.A. section not organised here, all mules, A.T. Carts + personnel for same in H.T. City of CALCUTTA. withdrawn. Brigadier AUDEBERT joined as interpreter.	MW

WAR DIARY

or

INTELLIGENCE SUMMARY.

(Erase heading not required.)

Army Form C. 2118.

Instructions regarding War Diaries and Intelligence Summaries are contained in F. S. Regs., Part II, and the Staff Manual respectively. Title pages will be prepared in manuscript.

Hour, Date, Place.	Summary of Events and Information.	Remarks and references to Appendices.
Nov 11th 1914	Disembarkation completed. At 2 P.M. marched to LA VALENTINE. Distance 10 miles where unit went into camp.	JW.
Nov 16th 1914	Left LA VALENTINE to entrain at D'ARENC STATION, MARSEILLES. 1st reinforcement & storeman (1 Havildar & 3 men) remained in camp, with Indians' surplus kits & column surplus baggage, to be handed in subsequently to Indian Base Depot. at MARSEILLES. European surplus kits sent with baggage of 8th Hussars to HAVRE. 1 sick horse sent to Base Vety. Hospital. 8 Boxes of Pistol ammunition for Carr Bde drawn from Ord'. Dept.'' Entrained at 3. P.M. Left D'ARENC Station at 4.5 P.M. Personnel complete, Horses 2 short of establishments.	JW/

Army Form C. 2118.

WAR DIARY
or
INTELLIGENCE SUMMARY.
(Erase heading not required.)

5

Hour, Date, Place.	Summary of Events and Information.	Remarks and references to Appendices.
Nov 18th 1914	Arrived at ORLEANS 1.20.A.M., (LA GRUE STATION) detained at once & went into camp close to station, 1 horse destroyed during journey from MARSEILLES.	
Nov 19th	Obtained 3 horses from ADV. Remount Depot to replace casualties, also 1 horse for Interpreter.	

Army Form O. 2118.

B Amm Col RHA

WAR DIARY
or
INTELLIGENCE SUMMARY.
(Erase heading not required.)

Instructions regarding War Diaries and Intelligence Summaries are contained in F. S. Regs., Part II, and the Staff Manual respectively. Title pages will be prepared in manuscript.

Hour, Date, Place.	Summary of Events and Information.	Remarks and references to Appendices.
Or'leans. Nov. 19th	Returned to Ordnance Depot La Chapelle. 180 Boxes of 13 Pr. Ammunition for the Amm. Park, of this 60 Boxes each was for C & G Amm Columns who have not yet arrived at ORLEANS.	NW
Nov. 20th	LIEUT. STEWARD, 1 Indian Officer, 6 Sowars & 2 followers joined the Column from the 6th Cavalry. Personnel S.A. Section.	NW
Nov. 21st	One Indian Officer 30 rank & file, 29 G.T. Carts, 59 Mules & 1 Pony joined as transport for S.A. Ammunition	NW
Nov. 22nd	24 rank & file, 24 A.T. Carts & 9 Mules joined as transport for 13 Pr. Ammunition C. & G. Ammunition Columns each received 60 Boxes 13 Pr. Ammunition.	NW

Army Form C. 2118.

WAR DIARY
or
INTELLIGENCE SUMMARY.
(Erase heading not required.)

Instructions regarding War Diaries and Intelligence Summaries are contained in F. S. Regs., Part II, and the Staff Manual respectively. Title pages will be prepared in manuscript.

Hour, Date, Place.	Summary of Events and Information.	Remarks and references to Appendices.
Nov. 22nd	290 Boxes of S.A. Amm. Mk VII drawn from the Ordnance Depot.	NW.
Nov. 25th	One European admitted into Base Hospt ORLEANS.	NW.
Nov. 26th	One European admitted into Base Hospt. ORLEANS.	NW.
Nov. 27th	Lieut Stewart reformed his regiment & Lieut Bickmore joined the Column on this date.	NW.

Complete up till Nov. 30 1914

[signature]
A.L. Indm
Capt
Cdg "B" Amm Column RWA

121/4246

War Diary of
"B" Ammunition Column R.H.A.

From 7-12-14
To 25-12-14
Volume I
Pp. 8 6-10

Army Form O. 2118.

WAR DIARY
or
INTELLIGENCE SUMMARY.
(Erase heading not required.)

"B" Ammunition Column. RHQ

Hour, Date, Place.	Summary of Events and Information.	Remarks and references to Appendices.
Nov. 7th	Entrained at LES MURLINS, station ORLEANS for HAZEBRUCK (Regulating Station)	AW.
Dec. 9th	Arrived at BERGUETTE, commenced detraining. 2 A.M. marched to AUCHEL where the unit went into billets. One Indian Driver two horses joined as part of refire transport. Two Gunners joined to complete European establishment.	AW.
Dec. 18th		AW.
Dec. 21st 11.6 a.m.	Ordr recd from Staff Captain R.H.A. 1st Indian Cav. Division for the Small Arms Section Brrne to move to proceed to VENDIN and support KBde Major SIALKOT Cavalry Brigade.	AW.
3.0 a.m.	Small Arms Section (LIEUT BICKMORE 6th Cav. Commanding) left AUCHEL	AW.

Army Form C. 2118.

WAR DIARY
or
INTELLIGENCE SUMMARY.
(Erase heading not required.)

B. Ammunition Column

Hour, Date, Place.	Summary of Events and Information.	Remarks and references to Appendices.
Dec. 22 5.30 A.M.	MAMETZ Rec'd orders from Staff Capt. R.A. to march at once to	AGW
7.0 a.m.	Rec'd orders from Staff Capt R.A. to move north at AUCHY-LE-BOIS and await orders. On arrival received orders to go into billets at LIGRES.	
2.30 p.m.	Proceed LIGRES and went into billets.	
Dec. 23. 7.45 p.m.	LIEUT BICKMORE with small arms section groups from E of BETHUNE where he had been stationed with the SIALKOT Brigade in support of INDIAN CORPS. The SIALKOT Cav Bde did not go into action, but ammunition was supplied to the Coldstream Guards and the London Scottish of the 1st Division which had come up with the 1st Army Corps to relieve the Indian Corps.	SEW
Dec. 24 about 4.30 pm	Rec'd orders from Staff Captain R.A. to be ready to move at a minute notice.	SEW
Dec. 26 2.30 a.m.	Rec'd orders from Staff Capt.R.A. to leave LIGRES in our billeting area at 10.0 a.m. (This change of billets was necessary to make room for the Indian Army Corps)	SEW

Army Form C. 2118.

10

B. Ammunition Column. R.F.A.

WAR DIARY
or
INTELLIGENCE SUMMARY.

(Erase heading not required.)

Hour, Date, Place.	Summary of Events and Information.	Remarks and references to Appendices.
Dec. 2.6.	Went into billets at ST HILAIRE	RW
General for month.	Note During the month December a contagion from of Influenza broke out among the horses of "B" Ammunition Column starting at ORLEANS. This was stated by the Veterinary officer not to be Pink Eye & a disease which was among the horses at ROUEN and also in the Veterinary lines at ORLEANS. Of this was correct this form of Influenza was probably aggravated due to the very muddy & waterlogged condition of the camping ground LES GRUES OF ORLEANS and the bad weather experienced there. When ORLEANS was left for the Vet. Hospits at ORLEANS, the remainder being kept with the column. Temperature in some cases went up to 106. W. in most cases fell very quickly & even in the worst cases horses recovered & were fit to work again after 3 weeks. Some in less than a week. but after symptoms often went cases was a considerable swelling of the legs + sheath heels & pubic neighbor. One Sergt, Lampis Sardeaux two pneumonia interpreted at LILLERS. Transportation died	RW

WAR DIARY
OF
AMMUNITION COLUMN

1ST INDIAN CAVALRY DIVISION

JANUARY – DECEMBER – 1915

(Feb. missing)

SERIAL NO. 283.

Confidential

War Diary

of

1st Indian Cavalry Division Ammunition Column

FROM 1st January 1915 **TO** 31st January 1915

Army Form C. 2118

WAR DIARY
or
INTELLIGENCE SUMMARY
(Erase heading not required.)

January 1915

Instructions regarding War Diaries and Intelligence Summaries are contained in F. S. Regs., Part II, and the Staff Manual respectively. Title pages will be prepared in manuscript.

Hour, Date, Place.	Summary of Events and Information	Remarks and references to Appendices.
January 1st	Still at BEAUCHAMPS MT.	
" " 6th	Inspection of Vehicles by O.C. A.S.C. 1st I.C.D. MT.	
" " 8th	The column was inspected in marching order by Lieut. Col. Charlton RHA O.C. 1st Ind R.H.A. Bde MT.	OK. 828 14/2/15
" " 9th to 31st	Exercise and Draught Parades MT.	

[signature]
CAPT. R.H.A.
COMMDg. 1st INDIAN CAVALRY DIVn. AMMn. COLn.

Serial No. 278

10/11/1719

WAR DIARY

"B" Ammunition Column R.H.A. 1st Indian Cavalry Division.

From 1st February 1915 — to 24th February 1915
28th

Army Form C. 2118.

B. Ammunition Column R.H.A.
1st Indian Cav. Div.

WAR DIARY
or
INTELLIGENCE SUMMARY.
(Erase heading not required.)

Instructions regarding War Diaries and Intelligence Summaries are contained in F. S. Regs., Part II, and the Staff Manual respectively. Title pages will be prepared in manuscript.

Hour, Date, Place.	Summary of Events and Information.	Remarks and references to Appendices.
Feb 1. 1915 to Feb 12	Marched from BORRE to VLAMENTINGHE. The Div. Amm. Column billeted in a farm 1½ S.E. of VLAMENTINGHE, 200 yards from the town in which Q. Battery have 4 guns in action 1½ miles S. of YPRES & their detachment here. The Column Ammn Wagons placed in the field where Q Battery's wagons were parked and ammunition transferred in required. Two wagons were sent up nightly after dark by Q Battery to their gun position to replace rounds expended during the previous 24 hours. No 50009 Gr. W. Arstall admitted hospital sick.	MW
Feb. 11. Feb 4.5 (night 10th-11th & 11th-12th)	A. Q. and U batteries handed over to Belgian Artillery 2 guns each night. On 11th the R.H.A. re'd orders to march STEEN- S. of AIRE. 1 Horse shot (by horse by kick from another horse)	MW MW

Army Form C. 2118.

B. Ammunition Column R.H.A.
1st Indian Cav. Bde.

WAR DIARY
or
INTELLIGENCE SUMMARY.
(Erase heading not required.)

Hour, Date, Place.	Summary of Events and Information.	Remarks and references to Appendices.
Feb. 6. 1915	2 Lt. A.G. TAYLOR R.H.A. & Lt. T.A. Stubbs (2 6/404) joined B. Section. Attached from 27th Battery R.F.A.	AW.
Feb. 12	4th R.H.A. marched to HILLHOEK. B. Section billeted for the night in a farm near ABBEILLE. (distance 12 miles)	AW.
Feb. 13	R.H.A. marched to BLEU - S. of AIRE. Ho. Dis. Ammn. Col. went into their old billets at ST HILAIRE (distance of march 28 miles)	AW.
Feb. 24.	No. 87902 Gr. E.S. Elkins joined from base. No. 51305 Gr. H. Gilbert appointed pinned a Br. to substitute 11 Feb 1915, transferred to Q Battery RHA, but remains attached to the unit.	AW.

121/5114

WAR DIARY

OF

Divisional Ammunition Column, R.H.A. 1st Indian Cavalry Division

From 2nd March 1915 to 31st March 1915

Army Form C. 2118.

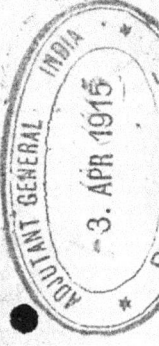

WAR DIARY
or
INTELLIGENCE SUMMARY.
(Erase heading not required.)

14.

Hour, Date, Place.	Summary of Events and Information.	Remarks and references to Appendices.
March 2. 1915	Lt A.G. Taylor R.H.A. taken into Hospital at LILLERS with damaged knee.	D.E.W.
March 3	One heavy draught horse destroyed, leg broken by kick. Rec'd orders as follows:— Div. Amm. Column, A.T. Carts + baggage togethr with baggage of 'A' 'Q' + 'U' Batteries & R.A.H.Qs to march to rendezvous at rly. crossing W. of MERVILLE leaving starting point BOURECQ at 6.0 p.m. Ammunition Wagons, Marching in rear of 'A' 'Q' + 'U' Batteries to leave starting point at 2.0 a.m. 4/3/15 to proceed to the same rendezvous. Both columns to wait at rendezvous till 6.0 a.m. 4/3/15 for the billeting party. A.T. Carts + baggage under Capt Willan R.H.A. left billets at 5.30 p.m. & arrived at rendezvous distance 14 miles at 1.0 a.m. 4/3/15 Batteries + Ammunition wagons left under Capt Whittaker R.H.A. at 1.30 a.m. 4/3/15 Small Arm Section arrived at ST HILAIRE	D.E.W.

Army Form C. 2118.

WAR DIARY
or
INTELLIGENCE SUMMARY.
(Erase heading not required.)

15.

Hour, Date, Place.	Summary of Events and Information.	Remarks and references to Appendices.
March 4.	80 boxes S.A.A. leaving here returned 2 days before to Amm. Park. There were now 8 empty A.T. Carts. Officer & went with the RMs sections on spare carts, the remaining 4 being left on spare with the S.A.A. sections.	DEW.
	Went into billets in farm 2 miles N. of MERVILLE at VIERHOUCK.	
	"Q" Battery went into action 1/2 mile S. of LAVENTIE 9 miles from VIERHOUCK. Firing battery & first line wagons left the hitting, but all battery horses took 8 or 9 mule teams 1 mile E. of MERVILLE. Ammunition supplied direct from ammunition column to Battery, column wagons going up for this purpose by night. Refilling point 2 miles S. of VIERHOUCK at TISSAGE.	DEW.
March 7. 4.0 p.m.	Rec'd orders at 4 p.m. to move to new billets on MERVILLE - HAVERSKERQUE road.	
	Left VIERHOUCK at 5.30 p.m. greatly delayed 2 miles W. of MERVILLE by meeting a brigade of infantry into their transport and the whole column did not get into new billet till 11.0 a.m. 8/3/15. 10 Amm. Wagons left for the battalion while the column was on the road, intercepting a supply column on a reserve road 2 wagons upsetting in deep ditch & could not be extracted.	DEW.

Army Form C. 2118.

WAR DIARY
or
INTELLIGENCE SUMMARY.
(Erase heading not required.)

16.

Hour, Date, Place.	Summary of Events and Information.	Remarks and references to Appendices.
March 8.	Everyone obs, therefore supplied. Amm. Column now in billets 2 miles E. of HAVERSKERQUE and 14 miles from batteries, entailing a night march of nearly 30 miles each time ammunition was supplied.	SW
March 9	R. of S. orders to move on 9/3/15 as follows:— Amm. Column to move up to billets at LA BRIANNE, 1 mile E. of MERVILLE where all except the 6 amm. wagons per section were to remain. The 18 amm. wagons to move to RUE DE PARADIS Rear R.A. H.Qr., then being adj. from 1 to 2 miles from all 3 batteries, at 12 noon. Horse teams & drivers legs both of motors cars	SW
March 10. 8 a.m.	Left billets to arrive at new billet at LA BRIANNE at 10 a.m. Capt White at 10 a.m. took all the 6 horse am; A, B & C batteries (the batter. captains leaving gone up to the batter. (motors) to RUE DE PARADIS. Capt Walker Riven left at 12 noon with the amm. wagons after column to same place. Battery horses in Column wagons placed in adjacent field N.of RUE DE PARADIS.	SW

Army Form C. 2118.

WAR DIARY
or
INTELLIGENCE SUMMARY.

(Erase heading not required.)

17.

Hour, Date, Place.	Summary of Events and Information.	Remarks and references to Appendices.
March 10th (continued)	R.T. Carts & G.S. Wagons remained at LA BRIANNE under LT. MC KAY RMA.	JW.
March 11th	To lessen the distances between LA BRIANNE & the RUE DE PARADIS, to 8 miles, a replenishing point was established in the Tram yard in ESTAIRES and 3 miles from the RUE DE PARADIS. 2 the place 30 A.T. carts under QMC IVES remained permanently being replaced by full ones as emptied.	JW.
March 13th	As a few shrapnel shells are exploding point in ESTAIRES this was moved back 1 mile to a field in the Western outskirts of ESTAIRES. NEUVE CHAPELLE, which (The fighting at & near NEUVE CHAPELLE, which commenced at 7.30 a.m. on 10/3/15 was now over.) No. 53165 Gunner R. Greening admitted to hospital sick.	JW.
March 15th		JW.
March 18th	Ammunition wagon returned at RUE DE PARADIS, & A.T. Carts returned at ST ESTAIRES returned to LA BRIANNE.	JW.

Army Form C. 2118.

WAR DIARY
OR
INTELLIGENCE SUMMARY.

18.

(Erase heading not required.)

Instructions regarding War Diaries and Intelligence Summaries are contained in F. S. Regs., Part II, and the Staff Manual respectively. Title pages will be prepared in manuscript.

Hour, Date, Place.	Summary of Events and Information.	Remarks and references to Appendices.
March 24.	Recd. Intimation that British personnel replaces Indian, on reorganisation of the 3 sections of 'G' into one Divisional Amm. Column on the British Expeditionary Force establishment, and arrived at Avesnes aux Bois.	
March 26.	Captain D.C. Wilson R.H.A. left for 'N' Battery R.H.A. G. Parker.	do
March 29.	Divl. Amm. Column formed on this date & B.C. & G. Amm Columns cease to exist as separate units	
Field 31-3-15.		

Capt R.H.A. Captain R.H.A.
Commanding Divl Amm Col R.H.A.
1st S.D.

WAR DIARY

OF

Divisional Ammunition Column, 1st Indian Cavalry Division.

From 25th March 1915 to 31st March 1915

WAR DIARY
INTELLIGENCE SUMMARY.
(Erase heading not required.)

March 1915

Divisional Ammn Col
1st J.D.

Hour, Date, Place.	Summary of Events and Information.	Remarks and references to Appendices
March 25. 1915	The Ammunition Columns "B", "L" & "J", which had for some weeks past been for the purposes of administration a Divisional Ammn Column, each self contained, to-day ceased to exist as separate units, and the process of organisation on the British Ammunition Column Establishment vide pages 74 & 75 War Establishment, began. The designation of the Column is now "Divisional Ammunition Column, 1st Indian Cavalry Division", and is composed as follows:— 1 Head Quarter Staff, 3 Sections numbered 1, 2 & 3, each Section being divided into 3 Subsections 'A', 'B' & 'C', 'B' Subsection of each Section being the Small Arm Ammunition Section. In the event of a battery being detached with its Cavalry Brigade, one Section would be sent to supply Ammunition. On the interim had part of the British personnel had arrived at Auchy Au-Bois:— Lieut Lo. S. McKay RHA, and two N.C.O's were sent to take over the personnel, Lt McKay to command the Small Arm Section, and to send up sufficient of the new personnel to complete two R.H.A. Sections.	

Army Form C. 2118.

WAR DIARY
INTELLIGENCE SUMMARY.
(Erase heading not required.)

March 1915

Hour, Date, Place.	Summary of Events and Information.	Remarks and references to Appendices
March 26. 1915	Capt H.A. Taylor R.H.A. was posted from Divisional Ammunition Column 2nd Ind. Cav. Division to organise the Column on the new Establishment & to take command. 2/Lieut C.S. Campbell R.H.A. arrived on posting from Home Establishment	
March 27. 1915	Personnel sufficient to complete two R.H.A. Sections was sent from S.H.A. Section to LA BRIANNE, excluding Non Commissioned Officers; which were as far as possible detailed from other units in the Division.	

Sd/
31/3/15

[signature] Capt RHA
Comdg Divl Ammn Col 1st I.C.D.

Serial No 283

121/5504

WAR DIARY
OF
Divisional Ammunition Column, 1st Indian Cavalry Division
From 1st April 1915 to 30th April 1915.

Army Form C. 2118.

WAR DIARY
or
INTELLIGENCE SUMMARY.

(Erase heading not required.)

Instructions regarding War Diaries and Intelligence Summaries are contained in F. S. Regs., Part II, and the Staff Manual respectively. Title pages will be prepared in manuscript.

Hour, Date, Place.	Summary of Events and Information.	Remarks and references to Appendices
April 3rd, 1915	Received orders from G.R.A. that the Divisional Ammunition Column was to move to billets to a village about half a mile East of LA GORGUE, in order to be nearer the Batteries in action should Ammunition be required	
April 4th, 1915	About 10 a.m., the Column moved from the billets in LA BRIANNE to the billets of 2nd Battery R.H.A., and took over the LA GORGUE, who moved out the same night.	
April 6th, 1915	Lt Colonel H. Rouse D.S.O., B.R.A. 1st Indian Cavalry Division, inspected the Ammunition Column in "marching order" about 8.30 a.m.	
April 8th, 1915	1 Fitter, 1 Wheeler, 4 Shoeing Smiths and 121 Gunners arrived from S.A.A. Section to complete European establishment. Instructions were received that sufficient Gunners had been sent to act as drivers, as there were no drivers available at the Base.	
April 10th, 1915	Authority was received to return the Indian Establishment until the European Establishment had reached the required Standard of efficiency, and to send the surplus Gunners above what were required for 3 Sections, to "A", "P" & "V" Batteries for training.	
April 12th, 1915	9.H. Gunners were despatched to "A", "O" & "V" Batteries for	

April - contd.

Army Form C. 2118.

WAR DIARY
or
INTELLIGENCE SUMMARY.
(Erase heading not required.) Divisional Ammunition Column 1st I.C.D.

Instructions regarding War Diaries and Intelligence Summaries are contained in F.S. Regs., Part II. and the Staff Manual respectively. Title pages will be prepared in manuscript.

Hour, Date, Place	Summary of Events and Information	Remarks and references to Appendices
8.45pm 24th April 1915 Rue du Dormier	Orders were received this afternoon for 2 Sections of A & U Batteries & 2 Sections of the Divisional Ammunition Column, to be held in readiness to move at 2 hours notice the remaining section of each Battery & the Column to remain in action.	
2pm 25th April 1915 Sylvester Cappel	The 2 Sections marched from Rue du Dormier at 8.45pm arriving at Sylvester Cappel near Hazebrouck about 3.0 AM 25. Marched from Sylvester Cappel to St Marie Cappel about 3 miles and formed up with the Colonne Small Arms Section, and the 1st Indian Cavalry Division.	
1.30pm 25th April 1915 St Marie Cappel	The whole of the 1st Indian Cavalry Division marched to-day. The other 2 Sections and Sistah Brigade Ammunition Brigade & Ambala Brigade. The Column marched immediately in rear of the Ambala Brigade. We arrived at our billet at "WATOU" about 6pm.	

Field
30.4.15

Walpole - Capt RHA
Comdg Div Ann Col 1st ICD

Serial No. 283.

121/5799

WAR DIARY
OF

Ammunition Column, 1st Indian Cavalry Division.

From 1st May 1915 to 31st May 1915.

Army Form C. 2118.

WAR DIARY
or
INTELLIGENCE SUMMARY.
(Erase heading not required.)

May 1915.

Instructions regarding War Diaries and Intelligence Summaries are contained in F. S. Regs., Part II, and the Staff Manual respectively. Title pages will be prepared in manuscript.

Hour, Date, Place.	Summary of Events and Information.	Remarks and references to Appendices
2nd May 1915	Received orders to march from WATOU at 8.30 am to ST MARIE CAPPEL. The column moved to ST MARIE CAPPEL as ordered arriving about 10.0 am. Received orders to march from ST MARIE CAPPEL at 2.30 PM to CRUSEOBEAU. The column moved to CRUSEOBEAU as ordered arriving about 6.0 am 3rd May 1915	
4th May 1915	Received orders to march from CRUSEOBEAU at 8.30 am to RUE - DORMOIRE. The column moved to RUE DORMOIRE as ordered arriving at 11.0 am	
4th May 1915	Received orders at 3.0 PM to BAC ST MUIR to march from RUE DORMOIRE BAC-ST-MUIR as ordered arriving about 4.30 PM.	
11th May 1915	Received orders to march from BAC-ST-MUIR at 9.0 PM to LOCON. The column moved to LOCON as ordered arriving about 3.0 am 12th May 1915	
12th May 1915	Received orders to march from LOCON at 10.0 am to ESSARS. The column moved to ESSARS as ordered arriving about 12 am	
18th May 1915	Minimum European establishment required to complete 3rd Station arrived with vehicles + horses	
21st May 1915	Received orders to march from ESSARS at 10.0 PM to WITTES. The column moved to WITTES as ordered arriving about 5.30 am	
24th May 1915	Received orders to march from WITTES to STAPLE at 8.40 am. The column moved to STAPLE as ordered arriving about 2 PM	

Army Form C. 2118.

WAR DIARY
or
INTELLIGENCE SUMMARY.
(Erase heading not required.)

Instructions regarding War Diaries and Intelligence Summaries are contained in F. S. Regs., Part II, and the Staff Manual respectively. Title pages will be prepared in manuscript.

Hour, Date, Place.	Summary of Events and Information.	Remarks and references to Appendices
28th May 1915	Received orders to march from STAPLE at 9.0 am to RUBROUCK. The column moved to RUBROUCK as ordered arriving about 12 AM.	
29th May 1915	2nd Lt. J. H. B. Ingley + 2nd Lt. C. Cromwell-Jones joined from base. Machine establishment of officers completed.	
30th May 1915	Interpreter 2nd Lt Carroll proceeded to ST OMER on transfer.	

[signature]

Serial No. 283.

121/6502

WAR DIARY
OF

1st Indian Cavalry Division Ammunition Column.

FROM — 1st June — 1915. TO — 31st July 1915

Army Form C. 2118.

WAR DIARY
or
INTELLIGENCE SUMMARY. 1st Indian Cavalry Division Ammunition Column

(Erase heading not required.)

Hour, Date, Place.	Summary of Events and Information	Remarks and references to Appendices.
8-30am July 10th QUIESTEDE	Received orders on the night of July 9th, to march at 8.30am July 10th from QUIESTEDE to WESTREHEM near DELETTES. Arrived at WESTREHEM at 11-30am July 10th 4 billeted.	

Field 6.8.15

CAPT. R.H.A.
COMDG. DIV. AMMN. COL.
1st IND. CAV. DIVN.

SERIAL NO. 283.

Confidential

War Diary

of

1st Indian Cavalry Divisional Ammunition Column.

FROM 1st August 1915 TO 31st December 1915.

Army Form C. 2118.

WAR DIARY
INTELLIGENCE SUMMARY.
(Erase heading not required.)

August 1915

Instructions regarding War Diaries and Intelligence Summaries are contained in F. S. Regs., Part II, and the Staff Manual respectively. Title pages will be prepared in manuscript.

Hour, Date, Place.	Summary of Events and Information.	Remarks and references to Appendices.
August 1st	Left DELETTES. Sections marching with their respective Cavalry Brigades.	BJT
" 4th	Arrived SURCAMPS. (SOMME) Sections joining up to H.Q. in billets.	BJT
" 7th	Left SURCAMPS & proceeded by march route to GORENFLOS.	BJT
" 12th	1 small arm section marched to CONTAY with the Sialkote Cavalry Bde & were attached to the 2nd & 3rd Car. D: Amm Col. A. & Q. Bys.	BJT
" 14th	Gun Sections of left with their respective batteries & marched to BRAY. (SUR.SOMME), went into action & were attached to 5th & 18th Div B.E.F.	BJT
" 23rd	Gun Section of "U" Bty R.H.A. marched with	BJT

Army Form C. 2118.

WAR DIARY
or
INTELLIGENCE SUMMARY.
(Erase heading not required.)

Instructions regarding War Diaries and Intelligence Summaries are contained in F. S. Regs., Part II, and the Staff Manual respectively. Title pages will be prepared in manuscript.

Hour, Date, Place.	Summary of Events and Information.	Remarks and references to Appendices.
August 23rd Cook	Battery to CHIPILLY, billetting for the night.	EJH
" 24th	Orders rcd by 3rd Section to march to BRAY (SUR SOMME).	EJH
" 25th	Section marched to BRAY, & were attached to 5th Division B.E.F.	EJH

Field
1.7.16.

E.J.Hpkins Lt Col
COMMDG. 1st INDIAN CAVALRY DIVNL AMMN. COL.

Army Form C. 2118.

WAR DIARY
or
INTELLIGENCE SUMMARY.

Sept 1915.

(Erase heading not required.)

Instructions regarding War Diaries and Intelligence Summaries are contained in F. S. Regs., Part II, and the Staff Manual respectively. Title pages will be prepared in manuscript.

Hour, Date, Place.	Summary of Events and Information.	Remarks and references to Appendices.
September 9th	(H.Q. & S.A.A. Sec.) Left GORENFLOS. for BETTENCOURT ST. OUEN.	GJK
" 19th	Gun sections from BRAY. joined up to H.Q at BETTENCOURT ST OUEN + went into billets.	GJK
" 22nd	Left BETTENCOURT ST OUEN. + proceeded by March route to MOUNT RENAULT FARM. (HEUZECOURT).	GJK
" 25th	Orders received to be ready to move at 1 hours notice.	GJK
" 26th to 30th	Billeted at MOUNT RENAULT FARM, under orders to move at 4 hours notice.	GJK

CAPT., R.H.A.
COMMDG. 1st INDIAN CAVALRY DIVN. AMMN. COL.

Army Form C. 2118.

WAR DIARY
or
INTELLIGENCE SUMMARY.
(Erase heading not required.)

October 1915

Hour, Date, Place.	Summary of Events and Information.	Remarks and references to Appendices.
October 1st	Left Mount Renault Farm + Marched to ST ACHEUL. (HEUZECOURT) went into billets.	[initials]
13th	Marched to MOUFLERS (SOMME) + billeted, two Sections at VAUCHELLES LES DOMART + one at MOUFLERS with H.Q.	[initials]
21st	Marched to LE QUESNE.	[initials]
22nd	Sections were allotted villages for billets as follows. 1st Sec. LE QUESNE, 2nd Sec. ST AUBIN RIVIÈRE + LEMAZIS, 3rd Sec + H.Q. ARGUEL. Remained in billets to end of month.	[initials]

Army Form C. 2118.

WAR DIARY
or
INTELLIGENCE SUMMARY.

(Erase heading not required.)

November 1915.

Instructions regarding War Diaries and Intelligence Summaries are contained in F. S. Regs., Part II, and the Staff Manual respectively. Title pages will be prepared in manuscript.

Hour, Date, Place.	Summary of Events and Information.	Remarks and references to Appendices.
November 19th	Ammunition Column inspected by G. O. C. 1st I. C. D. in Billets. (Report VERY SATISFACTORY)	[signature]
21st	Ammn Column inspected by Divisional Artillery Commander.	[signature]
23rd	Remounts & Reinforcements inspected by G. O. C. 2nd Ind. Cav. Corps.	[signature]
24th	Remained in Billets to end of month. PARADES :- Draught Parade, Marching Orders & EXERCISE.	[signature]

[signature] CAPT., R.H.A.
COMMG. 1st INDIAN CAVALRY DIVN. AMMN. COL.

Army Form C. 2118.

WAR DIARY
or
INTELLIGENCE SUMMARY.
(Erase heading not required.)

December 1915.

Instructions regarding War Diaries and Intelligence Summaries are contained in F. S. Regs., Part II, and the Staff Manual respectively. Title pages will be prepared in manuscript.

Hour, Date, Place.	Summary of Events and Information.	Remarks and references to Appendices.
December 8th	Gun Section of "A" Bty R.H.A. received orders to march with Battery to BRAY.	JH
9th	2nd Section left with "A" Battery, R.H.A. + were attached to 5th Division B.E.F.	JH
9th	3rd Section received orders to move with "U" Bty R.H.A.	JH
10th	3rd Section marched with "U" Battery R.H.A. + proceeded to ETINEHEM. + were attached to 18th Division B.E.F.	JH
15th	S.A.A. Sections + H.Q. + 1st Gun Section left LE MAZIS + proceeded by march route to BEAUCHAMPS. Arrived at BEAUCHAMPS + went into billets. remained in billets for remainder of month.	JH

J. Hopkins, Capt., R.H.
COMMDG. 1st INDIAN CAVALRY DIVN. AMMN. COL

SERIAL NO. 283

Confidential

War Diary

of

1st Indian Cavalry Division Ammunition Column

FROM 1st February 1916 TO 29th February 1916

Army Form C. 2118.

WAR DIARY
or
INTELLIGENCE SUMMARY. February 1916

(Erase heading not required.)

Instructions regarding War Diaries and Intelligence Summaries are contained in F. S. Regs., Part II, and the Staff Manual respectively. Title pages will be prepared in manuscript.

Hour, Date, Place.	Summary of Events and Information	Remarks and references to Appendices.
February 1st	Still at BEAUCHAMPS.	J.T.
" 5th	3rd Section having come out of action at Etinehem, arrived at BOUVAINCOURT at 3.30 p.m. and went into billets.	J.T.
" 8th	3rd Section was inspected in their billets by Col. Charlton, O.C 1st Ind. R.H.A. Bde.	J.T.
" 14th	2nd Section having come out of action at CHIPILLY arrived at BEAUCHAMPS at 2.30 pm and went into billets.	J.T.
" 15th to 29th	Exercise and Draught Parades	J.T.

Serial No 283

Confidential

War Diary

of

1st Indian Cavalry Division Ammunition Column

FROM 1st March 1916 TO 31st March 1916

WAR DIARY

INTELLIGENCE SUMMARY.

(Erase heading not required.)

Army Form C. 2118.

March 1916

Hour, Date, Place.	Summary of Events and Information	Remarks and references to Appendices.
March 1st to 25th	Still at BEAUCHAMPS Exercise and Draught Parades	
" " 26th	Left BEAUCHAMPS and BOUVAINCOURT at 9.50 am and proceeded by march route to NEUF MOULIN. arrived at 4 pm 26-3-16 and billeted for the night	
" " 27th	Left NEUF MOULIN at 8 am and marched to ST GEORGES arriving at 4 pm 27-3-16 and went into billets	
" " 28th to 31st	Exercises	

SERIAL NO. 283

Confidential

War Diary

of

1st Indian Cavalry Divisional Ammunition Column

FROM 1st April 1916 TO 30th April 1916.

Army Form C. 2118.

WAR DIARY
or
INTELLIGENCE SUMMARY.

(Erase heading not required.)

APRIL 1916

Instructions regarding War Diaries and Intelligence Summaries are contained in F. S. Regs., Part II, and the Staff Manual respectively. Title pages will be prepared in manuscript.

Hour, Date, Place.	Summary of Events and Information.	Remarks and references to Appendices.
April 1st to 14th	Still at St GEORGES	J.M.T.
" " 15th	Draught Parades and Exercises	J.M.T.
	1st Section and Head Quarters left St GEORGES at 8.30 am and proceeded by march route to MILLENCOURT for Training, arrived at 3 pm and went into billets.	
" " 16	2nd Section left St GEORGES at 8.30 and proceeded by march route to ARGENVILLERS for Training arrived at 1.30 pm and went into billets.	J.M.T.
	Brigade Training for 1st and 2nd Sections.	J.M.T.
" " 17 to 29	3rd Section at St GEORGES. Draught Parades & Exercises	J.M.T.
" " 30th	3rd Section having arrived at MILLENCOURT at 1.30 pm from St GEORGES took over billets of the 1st Section who left at 8 am and proceeded to permanent billets at St GEORGES	J.M.T.

J.M. Taylor
CAPT., R.H.A.
COMMDG. 1st INDIAN CAVALRY DIVN. AMMN. COL.

SERIAL NO. 283.

Confidential

War Diary

of

1st Indian Cavalry Divisional Ammunition Column.

FROM 1st May 1915 TO 31st May 1915

Army Form C. 2118.

WAR DIARY
or
INTELLIGENCE SUMMARY.
(Erase heading not required.)

MAY 1916

Instructions regarding War Diaries and Intelligence Summaries are contained in F. S. Regs., Part II, and the Staff Manual respectively. Title pages will be prepared in manuscript.

Hour, Date, Place.	Summary of Events and Information.	Remarks and references to Appendices.
MAY 1st TO 5th 6th	2nd Section & 3rd Section continued with Brigade training	
—	2nd & 3rd Section moved by route march to permanent billets (St GEORGES) leaving at 9 A.M. arriving at St GEORGES at 2.30 P.M. & joining up with 1st Section	
— 10th	left St GEORGES at 10 A.M. by route march for ETREE-WAMIN. arriving here at 3 P.M.	
— 18th to 31st	H.Q's & gun Section left ETREE-WAMIN at 9.30 A.M and proceeded by route march to MINGOVAL. arriving there at 2.15 P.M. attached to 51st (Highland) Division B.E.F. in action behind the VIMY RIDGE	
— 18th to 31st	S.A.A Section remaining at ETREE-WAMIN.	

CAPT. R.H.A.
COMDG. 1st INDIAN CAVALRY DIVN. AMMN. COL.

SERIAL NO. 283.

Confidential
War Diary
of

1st Indian Cavalry Divisional Ammunition Column.

FROM 1st June 1916 TO 30th June 1916.

Army Form C. 2118.

WAR DIARY
or
INTELLIGENCE SUMMARY.

(Erase heading not required.)

Instructions regarding War Diaries and Intelligence Summaries are contained in F. S. Regs., Part II, and the Staff Manual respectively. Title pages will be prepared in manuscript.

JUNE 1916

Hour, Date, Place.	Summary of Events and Information.	Remarks and references to Appendices.
1st to 3rd	Still at MINGOVAL.	
4th to 28th	Left MINGOVAL at 8.30 am. proceeded to FREVIN-CAPELLE arriving at 11.0 am	
4th to 29th	Remained at FREVIN-CAPELLE.	
29th	S.A.A Section's remained at ETREE-WAMIN. from Section's with Head Quarters left FREVIN-CAPELLE and proceeded by march route to ETREE-WAMIN leaving at 7 PM and arriving at 11.30 PM. and joined up with the S.A.A Sections.	
30th	The Column moved by march route to DOULLENS leaving ETREE-WAMIN at 12 noon arriving at 3.0 PM.	

[signature]
CAPT., R.H.A.
COMMDG. 1st INDIAN CAVALRY DIVN. AMMN. COL.

SERIAL NO. 283

Confidential

War Diary

of

1st Indian Cavalry Divisional Ammunition Column

FROM 1st July 1916 TO 31st July 1916

A.A.C.

Army Form C. 2118.

WAR DIARY
or
INTELLIGENCE SUMMARY.
(Erase heading not required.)

July 1916

Instructions regarding War Diaries and Intelligence Summaries are contained in F. S. Regs., Part II, and the Staff Manual respectively. Title pages will be prepared in manuscript.

Hour, Date, Place.	Summary of Events and Information.	Remarks and references to Appendices.
1st July 1916.	Still at Doullens	
2nd "	Left Doullens at 6 PM and proceeded by march route to BEAUVOIR-RIVIERE arriving there at 9.15 PM	
14th "	3rd Section left with "U" Battery R.H.A and proceeded to MEAULTE. Attached to 5th Division 4th Army	
18th "	The Column left BEAUVOIR-RIVIERE for ACQ at 8.45 AM arriving at 6.30 PM 2nd/Lieut W.K. Holmes R.F.A posted to "U" Battery R.H.A	
26th "	Remained at ACQ	
19th to 31st		

[Signature]
CAPT., R.F.A.
COMMDG. 1st INDIAN CAVALRY DIVN. AMMN. COL.

SERIAL NO. 283.

Confidential
War Diary
of

1st Indian Cavalry Divisional Ammunition Column.

FROM 1st August 1916 TO 31st August 1916.

Div Ammn Column

Army Form C. 2118.

WAR DIARY
or
INTELLIGENCE SUMMARY.
(Erase heading not required.)

August 1916

Hour, Date, Place.	Summary of Events and Information.	Remarks and references to Appendices.
August 1st to 31st 1916	Remained at A.O.Q (Pas de Calais) During the month	

Signed,
CAPT., R.H.A.
COMMDG. 2ND INDIAN CAVALRY DIVN. AMMN. COL.

SERIAL No. 283.

Confidential
War Diary
of

Ammunition Column, 1st Indian Cavalry Division.

FROM 1st September 1916 TO 30th September 1916

Army Form C. 2118.

WAR DIARY

or

INTELLIGENCE SUMMARY.

(Erase heading not required.)

September 1916

Instructions regarding War Diaries and Intelligence Summaries are contained in F. S. Regs., Part II, and the Staff Manual respectively. Title pages will be prepared in manuscript.

Hour, Date, Place.	Summary of Events and Information.	Remarks and references to Appendices.
1st September	Still at Ocq[?].	JFT
3rd	S.A.A. Section left ACQ at 6.30 AM and proceeded by march route to FORTEL arriving at 3 p.m.	JFT
8th	Gun sections and 'B' Q' left ACQ at 7.15 AM and proceeded to REBEUVE arriving at 3 p.m %	JFT
9th	Left REBEUVE at 8.30 AM & proceeded to BEALCOURT arriving at 1.30 p.m.	JFT
9th	S.A.A. Section left FORTEL at 7.15 AM & proceeded to BEALCOURT arriving at 12.30 p.m.	JFT
11th	Column left BEALCOURT at 8.30 AM and proceeded to DOULLENS arriving at 11.45 AM	JFT
13th	Left DOULLENS at 3.30 p.m. & proceeded to FRESHENCOURT arriving there at 9.30 p.m	JFT
15th	"A" Sub-Section left FRESHENCOURT at 5 AM	JFT

Army Form C. 2118.

WAR DIARY
or
INTELLIGENCE SUMMARY.
(Erase heading not required.)

September (continued)

Hour, Date, Place.	Summary of Events and Information.	Remarks and references to Appendices.
24th September	and proceeded to VILLE-SUR-ANCRE arriving at 3 PM.	MT
25th	Left VILLE-SUR-ANCRE at 6.30 AM and proceeded to MAMETZ Wood arriving there at 11.45 AM. Left MAMETZ Wood at 10.30 PM & proceeded to VILLE-SUR-ANCRE arriving at 1.30 AM 26-9-16	MT
26th	A Sub Section of 3rd Section left VILLE-SUR-ANCRE for MAMETZ Wood arriving at 5 PM & proceeded to MAMETZ Wood arriving at 8.30 PM.	MT
27th	A Sub Section of 3rd Section left MAMETZ Wood at 9 AM arriving at VILLE-SUR-ANCRE 12 o/c noon	MT
27	The A Sub Section left VILLE-SUR-ANCRE at 2 PM & proceeded to BUSSY-LES-DAOURS arriving at 5.30 PM.	MT

Army Form C. 2118.

WAR DIARY
or
INTELLIGENCE SUMMARY.
(Erase heading not required.)

Sept continued

Instructions regarding War Diaries and Intelligence Summaries are contained in F. S. Regs., Part II, and the Staff Manual respectively. Title pages will be prepared in manuscript.

Hour, Date, Place.	Summary of Events and Information.	Remarks and references to Appendices.
28th Sept	Left Bussy-Les-Daours at 9 AM & proceeded to Pierre-a-Gouy arriving at 3 PM.	J.M.T.
29th	Left Pierre-a-Gouy at 8:30 AM and proceeded to Cocquerel arriving at 1.0 PM	J.M.T.
29th	Heavy Section left Freshencourt @ 8-30 AM and proceeded to Cocquerel arriving at 4.0 PM joining remainder of Column.	J.M.T.
30th	Column left Cocquerel @ 8 % & proceeded to Raye-sur-Authie arriving at 4 PM.	J.M.T.

Captain
Co. 2nd A.K.A.

SERIAL NO. 283.

Confidential

War Diary

of

Ammunition Column 1st Cavalry Division
(late 1st Ind. Cav. Div.)

FROM 1st October 1916 TO 30th November 27th October 1916.

Army Form C. 2118.

WAR DIARY
or
INTELLIGENCE SUMMARY.

(Erase heading not required.)

October 1916

Instructions regarding War Diaries and Intelligence Summaries are contained in F. S. Regs., Part II, and the Staff Manual respectively. Title pages will be prepared in manuscript.

Hour, Date, Place.	Summary of Events and Information.	Remarks and references to Appendices.
1st October 1916	Remained at Raye-Sur-Authie	
2nd "	Left Raye-Sur-Authie at 8.30 AM and proceeded by march route to Estree-Les-Crecy arriving @ 12.15 PM	
3rd/10 31st	Remained at Estree-Les-Crecy	

CAPT., R.H.A.
COMMDG. 1st INDIAN CAVALRY DIVN. AMMN. COL

Army Form C. 2118.

WAR DIARY
or
INTELLIGENCE SUMMARY.

(Erase heading not required.)

November 1916

Hour, Date, Place.	Summary of Events and Information.	Remarks and references to Appendices.
1st November 1916	Remained at Estrée-Les-Creey.	
2nd "	Left Estrée-Les-Creey at 8:30 AM and proceeded by march route to VALINES arriving at 2-4-5 pm	
9th "	Left VALINES at 10 AM and proceeded by march route to Fressenneville arriving at 11-15 AM	
18th "	Gun Section of "A" Bty R.H.A received orders to march with Battery	
19th "	2nd Section left with "A" Bty R.H.A and were attached to 13th Corps 4th Army	
10th to 30th	Remained at Fressenneville.	

[signature]
CAPT., R.H.A.
COMMDG. 1st INDIAN CAVALRY DIVN. AMMN. COL

SERIAL NO. 283.

Confidential
War Diary
of

Ammunition Column 4th Cavalry Division.

FROM 1st December 1916. TO 31st December 1916.

Army Form C. 2118.

WAR DIARY
or
INTELLIGENCE SUMMARY.
(Erase heading not required.)

C O N F I D E N T I A L.

WAR DIARY
OF
4th CAVALRY DIVISIONAL AMMUNITION COLUMN

FROM 1st DECEMBER 1916 TO 31st DECEMBER 1916.

(VOLUME I.)

Army Form C. 2118.

WAR DIARY
or
INTELLIGENCE SUMMARY.
(Erase heading not required.)

December 1916

Instructions regarding War Diaries and Intelligence Summaries are contained in F. S. Regs., Part II, and the Staff Manual respectively. Title pages will be prepared in manuscript.

Hour, Date, Place.	Summary of Events and Information.	Remarks and references to Appendices.
December 1st to 31st	Remained at 'Fressenneville' (Somme) during month	

[signature]
COMMDG. 4th CAVALRY DVN. AMMN. COL.

[signature]
CAPT. R.H.A.

www.ingramcontent.com/pod-product-compliance
Lightning Source LLC
Chambersburg PA
CBHW081241170426
43191CB00034B/1999